The Un-Socialist Chickens

david culver brenner

Acknowledgements

This book was inspired by Catholic mystic and writer Caryll Houselander's story, "The Uncommunist Cow," from her delightful collection of children's stories, *The Animals in the Ark*.

I am deeply gratefully for the editorial contributions of Kristen, along with George Johnson and Cici Palme.

Dedication

For Kristen, Pierce, Luke, and Jeremy, whose laughter, encouragement, patience and support turn this hard-boiled egg sunny side up.

Table of Contents

Essays on the Perils of Socialism

The Un-Socialist Chickens

Religion that God our Father accepts as pure and faultless is this: to look after orphans and widows in their distress and to keep oneself from being polluted by the world.

James 1:27

The problem with socialism is that you eventually run out of other people's money.

Margaret Thatcher

Chapter 1
Sunday Visits

Feeding on freshly scattered corn and grain is a delight for any chicken, but it didn't fully account for Hattie's joy as she meandered around the pen seeking choice morsels. It was also the early fall morning with sunshine brimming, a soft wind scented with the coming autumn, and her best friend, Eunice, by her side. All the chickens at Peter's poultry farm clucked happily between gulps of feed, which to Hattie was a symphony.

Peter's approach to farming was old-fashioned, as was Peter, you might say. For one thing, he rejected the latest egg production techniques that were designed to speed up, through trickery, the natural egg-laying cycle. At the large egg factories, the lights in the chicken quarters came on early —well before dawn—and the chickens enjoyed less daylight once the sun came up. By mid-

afternoon, they were hustled back into dark barns, where "night" time also arrived early. And every day this routine began even earlier, so that nine days could be crammed into a single week.

Hens naturally produce one egg every day, but by shortening the days, they could be fooled into producing eight or nine eggs in a week. They suffered for it, though, and were tired, cranky, and miserable most of the time. Hens could only tolerate this schedule for a year or so, and when they inevitably became sick and unable to keep up, they were moved from egg production to a far worse and short-lived job: meat production, where sleep was actually too plentiful.

Hattie, Eunice, and their many hen sisters were widely known for laying the largest and tastiest eggs in the area, thanks to Peter's rich feed and gentle ways. This is how they rewarded Peter for his kindness. Even the three roosters in their coop, Chauncy, Clancy, and Beauregard, recognized their great good fortune to live on Peter's farm, and crowed heartily each morning in gratitude. And, despite their naturally competitive natures, the three roosters rarely pecked at or bickered with one another.

Most Sundays, Peter would load his cart with six or so dozen eggs and ride into the village. As the cart rocked back and forth along the bumpy road, Peter sang familiar songs to his donkey, which calmed and encouraged the animal. Gregarious by nature, Peter bantered freely with people and animals alike.

Peter's first stop was the small hut of an elderly widow, Irina, whose only child, a son, had died fighting as an infantryman during the Great War. Her husband, a skilled mechanic and handyman, passed away several years later.

Irina opened the door and smiled broadly. She enjoyed these visits, not only for the gifts of food that Peter brought, but also for conversation. "Peter, Peter, so good to see you, thank you for coming," she exclaimed, as she hurried to put water on the stove for tea.

"First come and take the food I've brought," Peter urged. Irina initially protested, but eventually accepted the food, telling Peter, "You shouldn't have." But Peter assured her, "I have much more than I can use, Irina — it will just go to waste — so, in fact, you are the one helping me." This was true, in the sense Peter's farm was quite prosperous; still, he could easily have sold this produce, but that was beside the point.

Irina beckoned Peter to sit at her small kitchen table as she hurried to heat water for tea and set the table with freshly baked rolls and butter. "Tell me, how is everything at the farm? How are your dear wife and children?" Irina asked with genuine interest. At one time, Peter's wife, Sonya, would accompany Peter on these trips, but the bumpy rides aggravated her sciatica, hobbling her for days afterward.

Happily obliging Irina's request for news, Peter told how his two sons, Dmitri and Leo, had given him eight bantam chickens for his birthday, all of whom were remarkable flyers and naturally high-spirited.

"They are smaller than most of my hens, and their eggs are likewise small. But they fly like eagles, Irina," Peter boasted. "Dmitri and Leo are always climbing to the top of the oak tree in front of our house to bring them down. I scold them, but they don't seem to listen," he laughed.

Irina, who was practical and less enchanted by animals, chided Peter, "You should clip their wings — that will keep them from flying away." Peter actually enjoyed the bantams' antics and flying prowess, so he just chuckled and told Irina, "Oh, they'll settle down once they learn our ways."

"Have you had any visits from Sister Tanya and her orphans," Peter asked. After Irina's husband died, Sister Tanya often came to visit her, with a few of the orphans tagging along.

"Yes, Tanya came yesterday with two new little ones — adorable little scoundrels that I had to chase outside, or they would have broken everything. After they'd tired themselves out, they came inside and we ate some of the cookies they'd brought."

Irina remembered that Peter's boys had come from the same orphanage. "Peter, it was so good of you to adopt those boys — they are such lucky boys," she said.

"Rather, we are lucky to have them," Peter replied. "Have you made these little rascals something to keep them warm for the winter months?"

"Their blankets will be ready by

Christmas," Irina said proudly. Irina had taken to knitting again, which she had always done for her own family, once the orphans began coming to her door. Over the years, she'd knitted dozens of soft, colorful blankets for the orphans, along with numerous mittens and hats. Each blanket was embroidered with a unique design and colors that included the name of each child in large letters. The children prized these blankets because they owned them, unlike most of their clothes and toys, which were passed on to younger children once they were outgrown.

An hour of conversation went by quickly, and Peter politely declined Irina's offer of more rolls and tea. "I must get to the orphanage, and home before it gets dark," he said.

After a visit to the orphanage, Peter planned to pick up a few items in the village for Sonya's Sunday dinner. After visiting with Sister Tanya at the orphanage and delighting the orphans with fantastic stories of talking animals on his farm, Peter began his way home, happily greeting friends and neighbors as he passed through the village.

This was a time to catch up, tell jokes, and laugh with friends, which he cherished—the villagers being almost as good an audience as his beloved chickens.

Once home, Peter excitedly shared all the village news with an expectant Sonya, Dmitri, and Leo, as Sonya began to cook the beef roast he'd brought from the village. Conversation would continue throughout the evening, as the four feasted on the succulent roast, along with Sonya's perfectly prepared potatoes and vegetables from the farm. Later, dessert and coffee were served, while story-telling, laughter, thanksgiving for God's gracious provision, and enthusiastic singing of hymns continued late into the evening.

Chapter 2
The Revenue Collector

Peter and his sons rose early the next morning, as they always did, to begin the day's work of tending the animals, weeding and fertilizing the crops, fixing fences, and maintaining all the farm equipment. They also chopped and split wood to feed the stove through frigid winters.

The calm of mid-afternoon was broken by the arrival of the Revenue Collector, Nikolai, for the monthly tax collection. Peter greeted him kindly, unlike most of his countryman, because he felt sorry for him. Nikolai, while disdained by the villagers, could count on Peter for sympathy and refreshment. He was invited in for a cold drink, bread, and cheese, and was soon basking in the warmth and solicitousness of Peter and Sonya.

Peter remembered that St. Matthew was also a tax collector before his calling as a disciple, and he showed the Savior's mercy to Nikolai, who was young and overly earnest. Nikolai admonished anyone who complained about taxes, which naturally made him unpopular. He'd grown more affable with Peter and Sonya, who patiently endured his occasional lectures on the responsibilities of citizenship and the deplorable attitudes of unpatriotic villagers who resented paying taxes.

When these same villagers begrudged paying their taxes, Nikolai thought to himself, "Who do they think pays for the guns and bullets and uniforms for our brave soldiers, who risk their lives to maintain our way of life? These grumblers will soon learn they've had it easy all these years."

Nikolai certainly shared the unbelief and general contempt toward religion of his University-educated peers, but he wasn't blind to its meritorious effects on the farmers and merchants he collected taxes from. Kind but simple men like Peter made his job easier, and far more pleasant, thanks to their infantile expectation of eternal reward or punishment.

Nikolai was no longer annoyed by the large crucifix affixed to Peter's barn and the hand-carved crafts depicting the life and passion of the Christ in his house. Nonetheless, he carefully avoided the gilt-edged bible, opened at the gospel of John, that was prominently displayed on a stand in the middle of the farmer's living room.

Nikolai had some important news to pass on this month, which he knew would not be welcomed by most along his collection route, which is why he'd chosen Peter to share it with first. It required some delicacy, though, so he began cautiously. He first praised Peter's sacrifice and care for the poor. Nikolai added that Peter's good works were widely known, even among the highest levels of government. This seemed impossible to Peter, but he merely nodded, not challenging such a far-fetched notion.

"Our leaders and your fellow citizens have recognized your exemplary example," continued Nikolai rather officiously, "and have graciously voted to adopt your compassion and generosity as a policy for the entire nation."

"How so?" asked Peter.

In response, Nikolai spoke the words he had rehearsed many times in his head: "Our nation will no longer allow our poorest and most vulnerable to suffer in abject poverty. It is our solemn duty as a prosperous nation to provide for their needs. It is wrong that so many luxuriate in the decadence of absurdly excessive wealth, while others have little or nothing."

His superiors had instructed him on introducing the new revenue collection policies, especially on the need to emphasize their great compassion.

Yet, hearing how wooden he must have sounded, Nikolai relented from his awkward formalism.

"Peter, no longer will the burden of caring for the poor fall on the shoulders of you and a few other like-minded citizens. Thanks to your leadership, our government is assuming the responsibility of providing alms, so no one will be without. We will collect enough grain, corn, eggs, milk, butter, and cheese to feed the needy and oppressed on your behalf. You will have more time to work your farm, without needing to undertake the burdensome trips you make every week."

Of course, this was not entirely happy news for Peter, since his weekly visits were the high point of his week.

But Peter accepted this as necessary because there were many widows like Irina. He also understood that there were many farmers and merchants who did not share from the abundance of what they produced. He could still check on Irina and Sister Tanya and the orphan children regularly, and bring whatever he could spare.

Having gained Peter's acceptance, the Revenue Collector loaded his cart until it was nearly overflowing, taking more of Peter's produce than ever before, and rode away. "Now," thought Nikolai, "if only the villagers are so cooperative."

Sonya, Leo, and Dimitri were silently dismayed that Nikolai had hauled away so much of what their hard labor had produced.

But Peter accepted it as God's will, and never grumbled. On this point, Nikolai was in general agreement, in that the government's plan was not to be questioned.

Chapter 3
Peter's Drudgery

Peter was now busier than ever, since keeping only half of the farm's production meant he had to work harder just to keep up with expenses. He had little time now to visit Irina and the orphanage, but at least the government was now providing for them, Peter consoled himself.

The orphanage was indeed getting plenty of food and solid gray blankets and clothes from the government, so they no longer needed Irina's blankets, hats, and mittens. Unlike Irina's colorful designs and soft material of combed yarn, however, government blankets and clothes were coarse and prickly, though warm enough.

Sister Tanya assured the elderly widow she was well supplied, so Irina stopped knitting. Moreover, the Revenue Collector had told Irina she was entitled to the government's support, and thus owed nothing to anyone.

She missed, however, the regular visits from Peter and Sister Tanya. The supplies brought by the Revenue Collector each month were appreciated, but he himself was usually brusque and hurried, having no interest in chit chat.

Meanwhile, Peter's chickens continued their work producing the largest and tastiest eggs in the province, although they noticed that Peter was not his usual cheerful self. Hattie and Eunice, more observant than most hens, saw that his steps had slowed, and began to hear sighs of weariness from him. Rarely did he sing the silly children's songs that so amused the chickens and lifted their spirits.

Beauregard, the rooster, who regularly perched on top of the coop to survey all that was happening on the farm, noticed that Peter was no longer making his weekly trips to the village. Meanwhile, the bantam chickens overheard the Revenue Collector's new demands of Peter, while sitting in the trees near Peter's house. Putting two and two together, Eunice observed, "Peter's spirits are down because he's no longer helping the widow and orphans. And, he has to work twice as hard just to break even — all because of that Revenue Collector."

The bantam roosters had also seen the Revenue Collector's cart, overloaded with Peter's produce, leaving the farm. Sensitive to Peter's low spirits, all the chickens resented the Revenue Collector. Hearing the bantam chickens describe how many of their eggs the Revenue Collector hauled away each week fed their dislike of him, even if Peter never complained about it.

"Where are all of our eggs going?" Eunice asked. A bantam chicken responded, "The Revenue Collector assures Peter that some go to the orphanage and some go to the widow Irina, since Peter always asks about them. But Peter doesn't know any other people his food is helping, and the revenue-collector doesn't seem to know himself. "I am not the only one distributing food and supplies," he says.

Eunice voiced the feelings of most of the hens: "So we are pushing out our best for people we don't even know."

"And it wouldn't be surprising if some of our eggs are eaten by the Revenue Collector himself," Clancy the rooster surmised.

Indeed, the Revenue Collector had begun wearing nicely tailored clothes, shiny leather boots, and a brass buckle on the belt around his growing waistline. "It seems he is being rewarded for collecting so many of our eggs," Clancy observed. Soon, their suspicions about the Revenue Collector were confirmed by wild birds that used to come by to pilfer food from the chickens' feeding pen, but were rarely seen anymore.

One day, Eunice yelled to one of these birds flying overhead, "Where are the rest of your friends? Why don't you steal from us anymore? We miss you," she teased. "We don't need your paltry pickings," the wild bird proudly squawked back. "We eat like kings from the Revenue Collector's cart. He doesn't bother to shoo us away like before—he's too busy sloshing down your farmer's rich cow milk."

This news aroused the anger of Hattie and Eunice, along with their hen sisters and the roosters. Even the bantam chickens, who'd only been on the farm for a short while, were furious, having already become intensely loyal to Peter.

Chapter 4
The Village People

Many of the farmers and merchants in the village also were incensed, after seeing the Revenue Collector take half or more of what they produced. They thought to themselves, "Why should we work like dogs all day, only to have our best efforts taken by the Revenue Collector?"

They too suspected the Revenue Collector of helping himself to their goods. Although not producing anything of value himself, he clearly was living quite handsomely.

A few of the wealthiest farmers and merchants did not complain, though. "We have more than enough. It is the least we can do for our less fortunate countrymen." Yet, they considered what the Revenue Collector took to be charity, fulfilling their obligations to help the poor.

Still, most villagers greatly resented the

government's new policy, and openly grouched about it.

And, while resigned to Nikolai's authority and demands, the townspeople soon realized that working longer and harder was futile. When they produced more, the Revenue Collector would take an even larger share. So, they worked less, and spent more time relaxing, which wasn't so bad. They had less, and filled their idleness with drinking and card games. Fewer jobs were available anyway, particularly for those without land or skills, so stealing became a practical necessity for many.

Naturally, less work also meant less goods for Nikolai to collect. Some of the villagers also began hiding their goods from the Revenue Collector, or trading them without Nikolai knowing. "The government is stealing from us," they reasoned, "so we must do the same to survive."

Nikolai, frustrated by their laziness, scolded, "The poor widows and orphans are suffering while you take it easy. This

will not do—you are robbing the needy and infirm." But the more he demanded, the less they worked, and his cart became lighter and lighter each day.

It wasn't long before the government could barely pay its soldiers and Revenue Collectors, much less provide for widows and orphans. Consequently, Nikolai now rarely brought food to the orphanage or to Irina.

When Peter learned about this, he was heartbroken, especially because he no longer had the means to help Irina and the orphans. All he could do now was pray for them, which he did faithfully.

Chapter 5
Broodiness

Morale among the animals was lower than ever. Peter's sadness weighed on all of them, especially Hattie and Eunice. So, the chickens started thinking and talking about how they could lift his spirits, or at least pay the Revenue Collector back for taking their prized eggs from Peter, which they also considered stealing.

"If we made more eggs for Peter to give away, that might make him happier," Hattie proposed. "But Peter still would have to surrender most of them to the Revenue Collector," protested Eunice. "Not if we hide them," responded Hattie.

"But, if the Revenue Collector found our hidden eggs, Peter would be in great trouble," objected Eunice. "Some of the wild birds have told us that farmers caught hiding produce are treated severely, lose their farms, and even go to jail, because they're guilty of defrauding the poor widows and orphans."

Hattie couldn't argue with that, but she also wasn't about to give up. She even stopped feeding for two entire days to talk to every chicken about what to do, for they were all distressed to see Peter so glum.

After not eating for two solid days, Hattie couldn't lay an egg. So, when Peter came in to gather the eggs that day, he was surprised to see that Hattie had not produced any. "I hope she's not sick," the farmer thought to himself, "she's one of my best producers." Before leaving the chicken coop, he blurted loudly, "Nikolai will not be happy about this!"

All the chickens heard this, and immediately an idea dawned on Eunice. She exclaimed, "That's it, Hattie! We'll fix that Revenue Collector and stop producing eggs! Chickens on strike! He can't blame Peter for that. Why should we work so hard just so the Revenue Collector can take our eggs and get fat on them," she exclaimed, proud of such a clever plan.

Eunice and all the hens, except Hattie, clucked loudly in agreement, resolving to stop their egg laying at once. When they had settled down, Hattie rebuked them for celebrating, and chastened them with sheer logic: "Yes, that'll fix the Revenue Collector. But it won't make Peter any happier. He still won't be able to bless the widow and orphans with our fresh eggs— that's what makes him happiest and helps him know his God is near."

"And," Clancy the rooster interjected, "Peter won't have any eggs, even for his own family."

Chauncey, the venerable rooster that rarely interceded when the hens gathered to talk, scratched the ground, the sign he was about to speak. All the chickens ceased their clucking to hear what the wise old rooster had to say. "The law requires that Peter give half of all he produces on his own land to the government," explained Chauncey. "If he happens to find our eggs in a nearby empty field, the Revenue Collector has no right to them, as long as Peter honestly believes they're not from his chickens. And, the field just over the fence behind our coop is vacant."

This raised many more questions, and

much confusion, but Hattie quickly grasped the solution proposed by Chauncey and immediately saw its main flaw. She asked, "How would we get the eggs to that field? The fence is four feet high and thirty feet from our hen house." Chauncey, as sharp as a hawk's claws, had already anticipated this problem and ingeniously solved it.

"If you'll roll your eggs to the outermost part of our feed yard, which will be easy since it's sloped downward, the bantam hens can grasp them between their feet and fly them over," he explained.

The bantam hens, until now silent observers, were elated at this idea. Speaking in their unique dialect of Chicken-ese, they enthusiastically agreed to the plan, for they had come to love the old farmer, too. "You can count on us, sisters and brothers. It is as easy as pie for us to carry the eggs over the fence," one said.

"Yes, we can fly just as high and far as any of those wild birds," boasted another, clearly exaggerating.

Their cooperation brought about a

great and joyous commotion, fluttering of wings, and wild clucking. But Eunice, skeptical as usual, wondered aloud, "How will Peter find the eggs we put in the field?"

"Perhaps we can draw his attention to that area with Molly's help," Hattie suggested.

Molly, one of the goats Peter milked to make the cheese that he and Sonya (and Nikolai) enjoyed so much, was known to hop the fence to munch choice greens on the other side. "Molly can stay by our eggs and bleat until Peter comes to bring her back–then, he'll see all the eggs we've gathered. Molly will be easy to coax into joining us, since she loves Peter, too," Hattie declared convincingly.

There was one more problem, which Eunice, not surprisingly, foresaw. She told everyone that Peter will be alarmed when he realizes he's collecting far fewer eggs from their nests. He'll also need to explain that to the Revenue Collector, she cautioned. Certainly, this was true, and it baffled the chickens for several days. Coincidentally, it was during this time that one of the hens became "broody" and stopped laying eggs. Hens will sometimes stop laying, and instead try to hatch non-existent eggs by remaining on their nests.

And this condition can spread quickly from one hen to another.

Here, right before their beaks, was the answer. Peter had already discovered one broody chicken, so he wouldn't be surprised to find more and more hens with the same condition. And, so common are broody chickens, even the Revenue Collector will not question it, especially since he knows Peter would never lie.

The chickens quickly decided that some of the hens would pretend to be broody by moving their eggs to the fence by the vacant field. Then they'd get back to their nests before Peter arrived to collect eggs. The bantams would carry the "missing" eggs over the fence and gently place them together in a pre-planned spot nearby, after which Molly the goat would stand by them and bleat for Peter's attention.

Once Peter discovered the eggs in the empty field, he'd undoubtedly give them to his widow and orphan friends. The chickens marveled at their own genius in hatching this ruse.

All the chickens happily agreed to the plan, and Molly was enlisted to direct Peter to the eggs. The chickens couldn't wait to begin.

Chapter 6
The Miracle of Eggs

A few days later, a third of the hens pretended to be broody by rolling their eggs from the coop down the gentle slope toward the farm's boundary fence. They did this as quietly and unobtrusively as possible, one hen at a time.

Once in place, the bantam hens took turns grasping the eggs with their feet, flapping furiously into flight, rising over the top of the fence, then slowly descending to a gentle landing on the grassy field below. They managed this task with great aplomb, transporting twenty-six eggs in less than an hour, only dropping and breaking two, which Molly helpfully slurped up, shells and all.

Then the bantams nudged the eggs further down the slope until they were nestled in a shallow depression under an elm tree about twenty feet from the fence.

Later that day, as she'd promised the

chickens, Molly hopped the fence and began grazing on a patch of weeds by the eggs. She chewed leisurely until Peter came within sight, and then began bleating for his attention.

Peter was not alarmed, thanks to Molly's habit of jumping fences, and he strolled over to the fence, enticing Molly with a sugar cube—which he carried for just such occasions. As he approached the fence, he caught sight of the eggs brand initially laughed at himself. "I must be seeing things," he thought, "or maybe my eyes are getting worse."

But as he got closer, he could see it wasn't a mirage. He could see the eggs were fresh and intact, and was astounded. "Where did these come from," he pondered aloud. No answer made sense, except one: The Lord had answered his prayers and provided eggs for the widow and orphans. Beaming inside, he collected the eggs, using his jacket to cradle them, and giddily hurried back to the house to tell Sonya.

Sonya gasped in amazement when Peter revealed the miracle; yet, even knowing of Peter's fervent prayers, she was hesitant to accept it as the Lord's work. "What should we do with these?" she asked. "They are not for us. They are for Irina and the orphans," Peter said assuredly.

Sonya, persuaded by Peter's unwavering certainty, and not wanting to disobey providence, responded, "You must leave this minute and take the eggs

to them. Far be it from us to delay the mercy of God." So, Peter quickly hitched and loaded the cart and hurried off to deliver the miraculous eggs.

Beauregard, watching Peter's discovery from his usual perch atop the coop, was ecstatic, and quickly shared with the rest of the chickens how their plan had succeeded. They clucked with delight, and the bantams put on a magnificent flying exhibition that evening.

The next day, just before noon, the chickens moved more eggs–over three dozen–to the spot where Peter found them, and Molly the goat again did her part by alerting Peter of their arrival. Soon, Peter was coming to retrieve the miraculous eggs each day without Molly's alerts. To avoid any suspicion, a different group of hens would feign broodiness every few weeks. Peter was never the wiser; besides, who would ever think chickens were capable of carrying out such a plan?

Chapter 7
Friendships Rekindled

Peter resumed making his weekly trips, with his cart loaded with eggs, to see Irina and the orphans. By this time, Irina was much in need, and visibly frailer. Of course, she was very happy to see Peter again, and eager to hear news of his family. She brewed tea for him, but at first could not offer cake or rolls. She'd been living on potatoes and vegetables from her own small garden, but now could trade some of Peter's eggs for oil, sugar, flour, and even bacon.

The orphans and Sister Tanya also were thrilled to see Peter again, especially carrying over twelve dozen eggs, more than the orphans needed. So, like Irina, Sister Tanya could trade some eggs and get much needed supplies and medicine.

With Peter's encouragement, Sister Tanya resumed regular visits to Irina's cottage, orphans in tow, carrying their familiar fresh-baked treats. Irina, delighted to see them, and anxious to bless the little ones, began knitting her colorful blankets, mittens, and hats for them once again.

As the weeks went by, the chicken's continued their routine, delivering up to ten dozen eggs to Peter each week. Peter stored them in a deep, cold cellar he'd dug to keep produce fresh until his next trip to the village.

Word of Irina's and Tanya's willingness to trade eggs became well known among the villagers, and eventually reached Nikolai as well. It never occurred to Peter, Irina, or Sister Tanya to conceal the miracle eggs, since they'd come from heaven and thus the government had no right to them.

Nonetheless, the eggs naturally aroused the curiosity and suspicion of Nikolai. "Perhaps Peter is once again supplying eggs to Irina and the orphans," he thought. And, despite his regard for Peter, he had to make sure the government was receiving its rightful share.

Nikolai first visited Sister Tanya, who

greeted him with her customary warmth and cheerfulness. "It's been so long since we've seen you, Nikolai–we've missed your visits. We thought you'd forgotten us," she said good-naturedly. Nikolai, feeling guilty that the government had stopped supplying food for the orphans, interpreted this as a complaint.

"We have not been able to help you as before, because our country is suffering a great economic collapse," Nikolai replied defensively. "Our farms and factories are barely producing enough to defend our nation, much less support the poor. We must pay our soldiers first, of course."

"Yes, of course, of course," Sister Tanya quickly responded, realizing that she'd touched a sore spot. "I understand our soldiers must come first. Besides, God has taken good care of us through his servant, Peter," she added. The Lord has miraculously supplied us with enough eggs to feed our children."

She described the story of Peter's miracle eggs, noting that Peter had discovered them outside his property. Nikolai, an educated man, listened respectfully to this fairy tale, but began to suspect that Peter's non-producing chickens weren't broody after all.

"Perhaps Peter would cheat the government to help Irina and the orphans, even though he didn't profit himself," Nikolai reasoned. "Even so, it is still stealing from the government."

Chapter 8
An Eggs-amination

Early the next day, a determined Nikolai set out for Peter's farm. Although surprised to see him, Sonya warmly invited Nikolai in for tea, as usual. But Nikolai, anxious to talk with Peter, refused.

"Peter is out working somewhere on the farm," Sonya told him. She could see from his curt manner that something was wrong. "I will go find him," Nikolai abruptly responded, and began walking along the fence that surrounded the farm.

It wasn't long before he found Peter repairing a fence post. "Peter," he loudly addressed the farmer, "I need to talk to you." Startled, Peter turned quickly, and, unused to seeing the Revenue Collector so early in the morning, hesitated a moment before answering. "Hello, Nikolai, it is good to see you. But, it is not tax time — to what do we owe the good fortune of your visit?"

Nikolai, while in no mood for pleasantries, wanted to avoid an ugly scene. "I was in the area, so thought I would drop by. In fact, I saw your old friends at the orphanage yesterday, and they send their warmest greetings. I am glad they are doing so well, thanks to you. Sister Tanya told me how generous you have been by providing dozens of surplus eggs."

Pausing momentarily, he continued, "But I wonder, with your broody chickens, how are you able to be so generous? And, of course, as you know, all of your eggs must be counted, so the government's rightful share can be collected."

Peter did not hesitate to tell Nikolai the truth of the miraculous appearance of eggs on the nearby field. "You see, Nikolai, my chickens did not produce these eggs, nor did they come from my farm. They were sent by the Lord himself."

Nikolai paused, considering how to respond to the old farmer's nonsense without insulting him. Finally, he asked Peter to show him the spot where the eggs were appearing each day. Peter confidently led Nikolai to the location, pointing to the flattened patch of grass not far outside his fence. Pointing, Peter said, "The eggs are right there every day when I come to collect them at two o'clock. This has been happening for many weeks now."

Nikolai speculated that Peter was the subject of a prank, perhaps carried out by his adopted sons. Nonetheless, he thought it best to accept Peter's story for the time-being, until he had firmer evidence it was a hoax. He nodded his head, and simply said, "This is very odd, Peter, but I have no cause to suspect you would make this up. But, as you know, I will have to investigate these unusual incidents, and determine what the government's policy is in such circumstances." Nikolai quickly said his goodbyes and left the farm, no less curious and perplexed than when he'd arrived.

Chapter 9
A Chicken Coup

Alertly noticing Nikolai approach Peter, Beauregard had quickly flown and hopped from his usual perch to a fence rail near where the two were conversing.

Eavesdropping, Beauregard became alarmed at the prospect of Nikolai investigating the appearance of the eggs. Immediately, he flew back to tell his fellow roosters, Clancy and Chauncey, both of whom agreed to call a meeting of the hens to discuss how to keep their secret from the Revenue Collector.

That night, the chicken coop buzzed with anxiety. The word had been passed from chicken to chicken, so by the time of the meeting, all knew of the Revenue Collector's visit and frightening promise to investigate their miracle eggs. The chickens of course wanted to save Peter from catastrophe. But how could they possibly thwart the Revenue Collector?

For several hours, the chickens grilled poor Beauregard on Nikolai's exact words, gestures, and even facial expressions to gain any insight into when he'd come to expose their scheme.

Hattie pondered this predicament deeply. Nikolai had not accused Peter of wrongdoing yet, she thought; he probably was embarrassed to accuse him of dishonesty.

Hattie, wise in the ways of humans, thus perceived that Nikolai would try to detect the secret unobserved. She confidently stated, "The Revenue Collector will no doubt spy on our drop-off location, in order to prove Peter is lying. But when will he come? That we cannot know."

The hens usually laid their eggs in the morning, sometimes as late as early afternoon, while Peter came at two o'clock to gather them.

"He will definitely be here by noon tomorrow," replied Chauncey. "He will want to arrive well before Peter comes for the eggs. No doubt, he will hide in the empty field to see who's bringing the eggs." This made perfect sense to the disconsolate chickens.

Hattie broke the silence when it seemed their heroic efforts were over. "We can't deliver the eggs, then — if the Revenue Collector sees us, he'll know we're only pretending to be broody, and he'll demand that Peter pay up on the government's share of our eggs."

"And put him in jail," Eunice dejectedly noted.

"Not delivering the eggs is no solution," Chauncey explained. "If the Revenue Collector doesn't find the eggs where Peter said they'd be, he'll think Peter's crazy, or worse, that he made up the story of miracle eggs just to cheat the government. Either way, he will be arrested."

While her sister hens moped, Hattie refused to give up. "What if we can convince the Revenue Collector it really is a miracle, and he has no right to those eggs?" she proposed. "That's impossible," a resigned Eunice replied. "He's an atheist."

One of the bantam hens angrily blurted, "I bet he's never seen flying chickens like us, though. If he saw us fly, he'd know for sure God exists."

Hattie mulled this grandiose notion momentarily, skeptical that the sight of the bantams' aeronautics could produce faith in the Revenue Collector. "Your feats of flying are truly amazing," she conceded, "but even they can't open the eyes of a blind man."

"Ahhh," Chauncey interjected, "but has the Revenue Collector ever seen flying chickens carrying eggs between their feet? And has he ever been pelted by eggs falling from the sky that explode and soak him with the finest yolks and whites?"

"That would certainly fill him with the fear of God. Besides, if we don't at least try, Peter will go to jail," the wise old rooster added.

Faced with such a sickening prospect, the chickens unanimously agreed that Chauncey's bombardment scheme was their only hope of saving Peter.

Chapter 10
Planning a Raid

Having arrived at a plan, the chickens furiously began their preparations. It was decided that all of the hens would produce eggs that next morning, and that they'd drop as many of those eggs as possible onto the Revenue Collector. They'd need to have the eggs ready for the bantams by noon, when they expected the Revenue Collector to show up.

The hens got busy laying eggs, while Beauregard kept watch for the Revenue Collector.

Once laid, the hens rolled them into position by the fence for the eight bantam hens to pick up. The bantams themselves rested that morning until it was time to make their bombing runs, since that would require all their strength.

The chickens worked hard from daylight to late morning, talking little. They were anxious to launch their attack,

and surprisingly unafraid. The prospect
of saving Peter consumed their thoughts.

The bantams slept soundly all morning.
By noon, all the eggs were in position.
The chickens finally were able to feed, but
the choicest morsels were saved for the
bantams, who would need great energy.

It was close to one o'clock, and the
Revenue Collector hadn't yet appeared.
Some of the chickens now worried that
their plan was for naught. "What made us
think he'd come back to spy on the field?"
Eunice doubtfully asked, "He can't really
believe eggs are miraculously appearing?"
forgetting that the Revenue Collector
suspected villainy instead.

"Of course not," Hattie responded, "But
surely he wants to know where the eggs
came from," she added. "He'd love to
catch Peter's sons moving eggs from the
coop to the field, and win approval, and
perhaps a promotion, from the
government."

Hattie's logic did not quell the doubts,
and the chickens fell silent, quietly
despairing they'd wasted their time.
Finally, Chauncey spoke up, "We can't be
sure he'll show up. But at least we're

prepared if he does." His calmness reassured the dispirited chickens, and their hope revived.

Chapter 11
Vengeance from on High

Beauregard, watching the field closely all morning, had gotten sleepy and sat down to rest, his eyes only half-open. If not for some wild geese that abruptly flew from the other side of the fence, honking as they went, he might never have noticed the Revenue Collector crouching behind a large rock near where the geese had startled. His sleepy state was broken, and he excitedly jumped from his perch, flying toward the feed yard. "He's here, he's here," Beauregard clucked — softly as possible so as not to alert the object of the chicken's wrath.

It was time. Two bantam bomber squadrons quickly lined up in groups of four. The first four would fly directly overhead and drop their eggs simultaneously, followed by the second

group twenty seconds later. They'd reload and return as long as there were eggs. The enemy was perfectly positioned in the open field, without cover, for a successful mission.

Eggs positioned underneath them, the first group deftly picked up one each between their feet, slowly rising into the air. The months of practice carrying eggs over the fence had prepared them well.

This time, though, they soared to the height of the tall pines beyond the field, eggs in tow, and glided toward the Revenue Collector, who was now sprawled lazily in the grass, waiting for Peter's "miracle."

Once directly overhead, the lead bantam clucked a pre-arranged signal, and three eggs came screaming down, one of them landing squarely on Nikolai's back, splattering yoke all over his clean white shirt. Unconsciously, he let out a loud grunt, and made the mistake of immediately looking up to see where the eggs had come from. The fourth egg, which had been released slightly after the first three, crashed into his eyeglasses, dislodging and knocking them into the long grass a good ten feet away.

Dropped from such a height, the exploding eggs stung Nikolai painfully, and gooey fluid sprayed in his eyes, temporarily blinding him. Dripping with the slimy liquid, he attempted to stand, but slipped in a puddle of raw eggs, sending him down hard onto the rock, badly bruising his ribs and hip. Suddenly, he heard the second squadron of egg-laden chickens bearing down on him. Nikolai, on his hands and knees, desperately searched for his glasses, groping among the thick grass.

His frantic search allowed the next four bantams, flying in tight formation, to pinpoint their target. They clucked in joyous anticipation as they dropped their payloads from over 100 feet above. Remarkably accurate, two of the eggs pummeled Nikolai on his neck and shoulders, and another smashed into his leg, causing him to wince in pain. He was now drenched in the sticky slime of raw eggs.

"I must be hallucinating," he thought, as he instinctively squinted at the sky to see if more chickens were on their way. He'd never seen chickens fly that high–and certainly not carrying eggs and dropping them with such accuracy. "How can this be? Chickens cannot be trained to do this," he thought.

Still frantically combing the ground in search of his glasses, the absurdity of the moment hit him. This was humiliating enough alone–what if Peter or his sons came by?

Then he heard more clucking above him. The first four bantams had reloaded and were making a beeline toward him.

Nikolai abandoned the search for his glasses, and began to run toward the grove of pines he'd come through on his way to the field. But he'd noticed the chickens too late, and even a moving target was no obstacle for the laser-eyed bantams. They expertly released their payloads in the Revenue Collector's path, scoring two more devastating hits—one to his nose and mouth— painfully dropping the frenzied tax man to the ground. He inadvertently swallowed a mouthful of raw egg, and began gagging and choking on the mucous-like substance.

Moaning and gasping for breath, he slowly raised himself and lumbered toward the pines, while the next group of dead-eyed bantams zeroed in. Four more egg missiles came screaming down, several landing squarely on his back and rear, again inflicting stinging pain and further coating him in the slimy substance of raw eggs.

Finally, the Revenue Collector reached the tree line, and hurled himself to safety under the tall pines. He had to hold back tears of pain and exasperation: He'd been disgraced and humiliated by chickens!

Covered head to foot by pine needles plastered to him by the glue-like eggs, the battered Revenue Collector didn't move for a long time. Perhaps God himself had been leaving those eggs in the field, after all, and had commissioned poultry to rebuke him for his unbelief, he imagined.

Yet, that very thought filled Nikolai with self-loathing—that he, an educated man, could entertain such foolishness. Still, there was no rational explanation for the degrading egg-pelting he'd just endured.

There was nothing to do except to pretend he'd never learned of Peter's inexplicable discovery of eggs. Telling his superiors in the government about it would only make him a laughingstock.

Anyway, he still had no evidence of wrongdoing, and the aerial assault—by chickens, no less!—had lowered his suspicions. Moreover, the mere thought of anyone finding out what had just happened made him cringe in embarrassment. He couldn't forget the whole matter soon enough.

With harvest season past, Peter was able to make more frequent visits to Irina and the orphanage, at least while the weather was agreeable. More than ever, his egg gifts were vital to their survival, as the government had ceased providing food and supplies altogether, given the country's ever-worsening economic conditions. So, Irina, Sister Tanya, the orphans, and Peter spent much time together, and their friendships deepened.

Hattie, Eunice, Chauncey and all the other chickens, who were responsible for supplying the eggs that helped the orphans and Irina to survive during this time of great want, were richly rewarded each day with Peter's cheerful banter and happy singing of their favorite songs.

And the bantam chickens, who received much praise for their heroic feats of egg delivery, felt certain that they were as fearsome and skilled at flying as the mighty eagle.

The End

Study Questions

Chapter One

1. Peter personally delivers produce from his farm to the poor widow and orphans he's befriended. How does his generosity differ from the way governments make welfare payments to needy citizens?

2. What is Irina's motivation for knitting blankets, mittens, and hats for the orphan children? How does her motivation affect the care and detail she puts into knitting them?

3. Do you think Peter considers his trips to provide goods to Irina and the orphans as a duty? Do you think he resents having to give away some of his produce? Why or why not?

Chapter Two

1. Is the Revenue Collector's attitude toward the villagers who resent paying taxes justified? Why or why not?

2. How much money is it reasonable for the government to require citizens to pay in taxes? Does 50 percent seem reasonable?

3. Do the governments of prosperous nations have a "solemn duty" to provide for needy citizens?

4. Do you agree with the Revenue Collector that the government's new plan is compassionate?

Chapter Three

1. Why do you think the government's blankets for the orphans are "solid gray" and "coarse and prickly," while Irina's are soft and colorful?

2. Eunice complains that the hens are producing their best eggs for people they don't know. How do you think most people feel about paying high taxes to support welfare programs, when they don't actually know the people they're helping?

3. Do people generally feel empathy for welfare recipients? Why or why not?

4. Why might the Revenue Collector and other government officials be wasteful of, or even steal from, the taxes paid by their fellow citizens?

Chapter Four

1. Why did the wealthier villagers feel that paying taxes fulfilled their obligations to the poor? How does paying high taxes to support welfare programs affect whether and how much people give out of their own "pockets" to help the poor?

2. Why did many villagers work less hard once they had to pay more in taxes? What did some villagers end up doing instead of working?

3. How did higher tax rates actually result in less money for the government? Why do lower tax rates often generate the same amount of or more in tax revenues than higher tax rates?

Chapter Five

1. Why was Hattie's idea to produce more eggs for Peter rejected?

2. Why was Eunice's proposal to go on a "chicken strike" impractical and unhelpful to Peter?

3. Instead of an income tax, which taxes work and productivity, what ways can governments raise revenue without deterring work and productivity?

Chapter Six

1. When taxes are very high, people will try to hide their income and wealth from being taxed. How do governments make sure that all income and profits are taxed?

2. What are some of the ways people try to prevent their money from being taxed?

3. What do you think is meant by the term, "underground economy?"

4. If the government taxed consumption via a sales tax, instead of taxing work and income, how would productivity be affected? How would savings be affected?

Chapter Seven

1. How did the government's new program to help the needy eventually affect Irina and the orphans? Were they better or worse off than before the government's plan began?

2. How did the Revenue Collector discover that Peter had extra eggs to give away? Would any of the villagers have a motivation to report Peter to the Revenue Collector?

3. What role might the government's new tax plan have played in the great economic collapse the country experienced? Is it surprising it can barely pay its soldiers and revenue collectors, and has no money to help the poor?

Chapter Eight

1. What did the Revenue Collector need to do in order to investigate and verify Peter's story?

2. Why does taxing productivity—the income and profits from work—require a large government bureaucracy?

3. The U.S. government collects money earned by workers in the U.S. before they ever see it. How does it do that? Does that make workers more or less conscious of the tax burden imposed by the government?

Chapter Nine

1. Socialist regimes have often been hostile to people of faith and churches. Why would socialist governments feel threatened by people's religious beliefs and activities?

2. Democratic socialism is often more attractive in countries where the majority does not believe in God or attend church. Why do you think that is so?

Chapter Ten

1. What effect might welfare benefits have on its recipients? Why would recipients be willing to accept money and benefits they hadn't earned?

2. Welfare benefits are often referred to as "entitlements." What does that communicate to applicants for welfare assistance?

3. What could happen in a society when it is split between those who support others by paying taxes and the people that receive those benefits? Will the society be unified?

Chapter Eleven

1. How did the government's new tax and welfare plan affect the relationships between Peter, Irina, Sister Tanya and the orphans? Were they stronger or weaker after this plan?

2. There is strong evidence that welfare benefits for single mothers weaken marriage and fatherhood. How might these benefits influence a woman's decision to have children and marry the father of the children?

3. How do social welfare programs undermine interdependence in families and communities? How does that hurt society?

Essays on the Perils of Socialism

The Inescapable Law of Human Existence that Socialists Just Don't Get

If we could wave a magic wand and implant one nugget of wisdom into the hearts and minds of our policymakers and leaders, it would be this: Whatever you reward, you get more of; and whatever you punish, you get less of. Every parent is well acquainted with this truism. Tell Junior that every time his bedroom floor is spotless by dinner time, he will earn a cookie; but that he will instead forfeit a cookie for every toy or article of clothing that's left on his floor by dinner. Query: Will the number of articles on his bedroom floor at dinner time increase or decrease after this system is implemented?

If you said, "decrease," kudos to you. You have mastered one of the most basic and inescapable laws of human existence. And, it is just as true for 10-year-olds as it is for 87-year-olds. Indeed, no self-respecting economist would dare deny that financial and other incentives powerfully influence and shape behavior.

This reality flows from a simple truth: we naturally desire to be richer rather than poorer, more comfortable rather than less comfortable, healthier rather than sicker, smarter rather than dumber, handsomer rather than uglier, and so on and so forth.

There may appear to be contrary examples, but they really aren't exceptions at all. For instance, some folks are content to be dumb because they love something more than being smart, such as money and power–e.g., reality TV stars, diet pill pitchmen, high-cliff divers, and yes, socialist politicians. In truth, virtually everything we do is a response to an incentive or disincentive for a monetary, material, relational, emotional, or spiritual reward or penalty. At bottom, we are all chasing the mechanical bunny, or running from the mechanical fox.

To want, and to strive for what we want, is to be human. Socialists and progressives seem to forget that the desire to make money and avoid poverty is the engine that makes economies run.

Whenever governments mess with this basic principal by diminishing incentives for work and initiative, or weakening disincentives for idleness and complacency, bad stuff happens. Indeed, welfare assistance provides food and medical care for poor families and children. That's what liberals see (God bless 'em!). But they never see beyond that; they never see how or why government charity nourishes the soul-crushing attitudes and behaviors that lead to and habituate poverty.

Sadly, many of our representatives in Washington, D.C appear to be oblivious to this fundamental principle to our nation's great detriment. Wealth redistribution through government entitlement and anti-poverty programs all too often have the perverse impact of generating even greater poverty and human misery, not to mention their tendency to corrode family, community, and faith-based relationships and influences that are crucial "seedbeds of virtue" in a free society.

Welfare benefits certainly will not make you rich–far from it. But, paltry government subsidies impede hustle in one important way that often is vastly underestimated: it affords leisure time. Most folks, including the illustrious staff at *ProofsandSpoofs.com*, strangely prefer relaxation to spending eight hours a day with a boss who usually isn't as warm and fuzzy as a terry cloth robe, fur-lined slippers, and a comfy couch. Progressive scholars tend to overlook what most regular folk like us have known for a long time: Leisure time rocks!

If you think we exaggerate, consider these disturbing changes since America under President Lyndon Johnson established the Great Society social welfare program in 1964. In his "report card" on this grand initiative 50 years later[1], Political Economist Nicholas Eberstadt verifies the late Democratic Senator Daniel Patrick Moynihan's concern over a consequent "tangle of pathologies" that Great Society welfare subsidies posed for African American families. As it turns out, the "tangle" morphed into something far broader and racially indiscriminating than he ever imagined[2].

In great detail, Eberstadt demonstrates that Great Society programs preceded the following:

- Nearly a third of Americans (32.3 percent) applying for and being dependent on means-tested welfare programs by 2012. Of the 90 million Americans receiving these benefits, only 33 million were deemed poor[3];

Nicholas Eberstadt, "The Great Society at 50: What LBJ wrought." *The Weekly Standard,* May 19, 2014, 29.

[2] Ibid., p. 28.

[3] Ibid., p. 28

- Men abandoning the labor market altogether in droves: the proportion of men ages 35-44 dropping out of work more than tripled between 1964 and 2014. And not due to unemployment—Eberstadt notes that, "For every adult man who is between jobs and looking for new work, more than five are neither working nor looking for employment.[4]"

- Births to unmarried women growing from 7.7 percent in 1965 to over 40 percent today, and the Census Bureau reporting in 2009 that only 57 percent of American children lived with their married biological parents, compared to 88 percent of children in 1960[5].

In short, exponential growth of America's welfare state has coincided with exponential growth in the tangle of pathologies Moynihan partly prophesied.

---

[4] Ibid., p. 29.
[5] Ibid., pp. 30-31.

Is it causation or merely correlation? Nicholas Eberstadt exercises restraint on this question, but notes the original short-term aims of the Great Society are irreconcilable with today's reality:

> Dependence on government relief, in its many modern versions, is more widespread today, and possibly also more habitual, than at any time in our history. To make matters worse, such aid has become integral to financing lifestyles and behavioral patterns plainly destructive to our commonwealth—and on a scale far vaster than could have been imagined in an era before such antipoverty aid was all but unconditionally available[6].

Ultimately, a misguided view of human nature is to blame for the failure to understand that giving someone something for nothing tends to ensure more of "nothing." If people were fundamentally good and would never opt for welfare as long as they could work,

---

[6] Ibid., p. 32.

socialism might be feasible. But common sense and history strongly say otherwise. Most of us are essentially lazy and greedy, and more than willing to accept stuff we didn't earn. Merchants know this well. And so, they coax us into buying their wares by first enticing us with freebies.

In the name of compassion, progressive politicians play Santa Claus, and in the process undermine effort and initiative, as well as the bonds of family and friendship, all of which are indispensable ingredients for a successful life, not just in a capitalist society, but in any society.

Just ask Junior, who has noticed that his cookie consumption has risen in direct proportion to his room getting tidier. If only Uncle Sam were that smart.

Welfare, Marriage, and Poverty

Were our legislators able to comprehend and honor the power of financial and leisure time "carrots and sticks," immeasurable heartache and suffering would have been avoided, particularly since the 1960's, when Uncle Sam began incentivizing unwed childbearing with utterly disastrous results for children and families.

Government itself is substantially responsible for a major cause of economic inequality and poverty in America: family fragmentation.

In 1964, when means-tested welfare for families with children became available via War on Poverty legislation, only 7 percent of children were born to unwed parents. Fast forward to 2013: 41 percent of children are born to unwed parents, and 68 percent of poor families are headed by a single parent, as opposed to only 36 percent when the War on Poverty began.[7]

Is the quantum growth in unwed births and poverty among single parent families solely the result of these welfare programs? No, clearly other cultural forces were at play–including the radical change in sexual mores since the 1960's.

---

[7] Rector, Robert. How Welfare Undermines Marriage and What to Do About It. Washington, D.C.: The Heritage Foundation, 2014. Accessed December 17, 2019. http://thf_media.s3.amazonaws.com/2014/pdf/IB4302.pdf.

As noted above, this certainly is not the only example of the government's failure to heed the principle that you inevitably get more of the thing you subsidize, but perhaps is the most distressing, given the monumental human cost it has exacted.

At bottom, socialism and welfare-statism fly in the face of human nature, and so produce unintended consequences that amplify suffering, not reduce it. Nonetheless, insight and humility are in short supply among our superhero politicians who insist on saving us, regardless of how much it hurts.

God or Government?

If you thought the problem of an over-sized and over-reaching government only applies to modern-day welfare states and socialist regimes, think again. It's an age-old problem that was just as real in ancient Israel as it is today.

The prophet Samuel exhorted the people of Israel to be content with God as their King at the time in Israel's history when power was diffused among local and decentralized "judges," a form of governance we might equate to federalism. In essence, Samuel warned them of the dangers of big government:

> Samuel told all the words of the Lord to the people who were asking him for a king. He said, "This is what the king who will reign over you will claim as his rights: He will take your sons and make them serve with his chariots and horses, and they will run in

front of his chariots. Some he will assign to be commanders of thousands and commanders of fifties, and others to plow his ground and reap his harvest, and still others to make weapons of war and equipment for his chariots. He will take your daughters to be perfumers and cooks and bakers. He will take the best of your fields and vineyards and olive groves and give them to his attendants. He will take a tenth of your grain and of your vintage and give it to his officials and attendants. Your male and female servants and the best of your cattle and donkeys he will take for his own use. He will take a tenth of your flocks, and you yourselves will become his slaves. When that day comes, you will cry out for relief from the king you have chosen, but the Lord will not answer you in that day."

But the people refused to listen to Samuel. "No!" they said. "We want a king over us. Then we will be like all the other nations, with a king to lead us and to go out before us and fight our battles." When Samuel heard all that the people said, he repeated it before the Lord.
The Lord answered, "Listen to them and give them a king." *(1 Samuel 8:10-22)*

So, Israel ignored Samuel's advice and demanded a real king like all the other nations had. Apparently, Israelite parents never chastened their kids with, "If all the other nations jumped off a cliff, would you do it, too?"

Samuel was personally offended by their obstinance, but God told him to get over himself–the people were in fact rejecting Him, not Samuel.

Faith and Big Government: An Inverse Relationship?

The Israelites rejected God in favor of government, which seems to parallel America's bent over the last half dozen decades. Indeed, the growth of government appears to be inversely related to faith in God, which has been declining over the same period.

We, like ancient Israel, are finding out the hard way that the refusal to embrace and conform to God's ordering of social, political, and economic relationships reaps painful results. Sadly, simple majorities in democratic nations can just as foolishly embrace government profligacy as can autocrats. So, don't take it so hard, Samuel. The same fantasies of a government savior persist to this day.

Christian theology affirms that the opposite of true religion isn't atheism, despite the claims of atheism's "adherents." When the heart relinquishes God, ineluctably it adopts a replacement, such as, for instance, a government that satisfies all our needs, thereby investing politics with existential importance. But, as God warned the Israelites, putting one's faith in government tends to hurt in the end, as the history of socialism makes clear.

Indeed, when government becomes an idol, tyranny necessarily follows. We are not there yet, but America has no absolute immunity from such an outcome.

Sphere Sovereignty and the Unique Challenges Faced by Christians in a Democracy

If you're a Christian who is against government welfare for the needy, expect some grief from fellow Christians as well as unbelievers. Since Jesus urged his followers to care for, "the least of these," when Christians reject government welfare policies, they're denying Christ and being hypocritical, right?

Such is the quandary for believers living in democracies who must negotiate two separate and often confused spheres. As individuals, Christians are called to help the poor. We are also, as citizens in a democracy, rulers of a nation—each of us is a, "little king," sharing power with many other little kings. In scripture, however, the role of the individual and the role of the state are quite different.

Evangelical Christians understand and interpret the Bible as the infallible and authoritative word of God, and as a comprehensive statement embodying all that is necessary for "faith and life." The message of scripture, moreover, is revealed expressly through its words, yet also through what may be deduced as the "good and necessary consequence" of those words.[1]

As either expressly revealed or deduced from holy scripture, God has instituted marriage, family, the church, and government and assigned to each of these institutions different privileges and responsibilities. God has also ordered their functions in a complementary fashion so as to maximize human thriving. For instance, married couples are to, "be fruitful and multiply." It seems the U.S. government has mistakenly taken this imperative to heart! Rather, the government is to maintain order by deterring and punishing evil.

Individuals therefore are not to take the law into their own hands. And, while individuals are called to love and forgive their enemies, the state must dutifully prosecute evildoers. If a Christian judge, out of personal compassion, forgives and sets a convicted murderer free, he has

---

[1] Westminster Confession, Chapter I, Section V

failed to act biblically–he has violated the separation of the individual and state. The biblical idea of distinct roles for individuals, families, the church, and the state is known as "sphere sovereignty," a framework articulated and championed by Abraham Kuyper, a 19th century Dutch pastor and theologian.

The "Two Hats" Believers Must Wear in Democratic Societies

Thus, democracy creates a unique predicament for Christians, because they find themselves carrying out two distinct roles and wearing two separate "hats." As individuals, they are to imitate the character of God by submitting to His laws–loving God and neighbor, as well as sharing the good news of Christ's redemptive work. Among other things, this entails the duty to "act justly, to love mercy, and to walk humbly with your God." (Micah 6:8) These mandates enjoin individuals and, by extension, the church collectively.

Separately, as citizens in a self-governing society, Christians, as noted, also are little kings, possessing the power and privilege of participating in governance. But for many unbelieving observers and Christians themselves, this is where things get messy and confusing. Should an individual Christian acting in his or her role as an architect of public policy help pass laws that dispossess an individual of their home and property for failing to keep up with rent or mortgage payments?

Wouldn't that be siding with heartless financial institutions? Indeed, an individual Christian, who owns an apartment building, might choose to graciously extend time to a tenant whose rent is overdue. But as "ruler," this same Christian must enact and enforce laws that are fair to landowners and tenants as well as banks and borrowers. People and entire economies depend upon such laws.

Likewise, as noted, a Christian ruler is called to punish and deter evil-doers, because that in fact is the state's biblical calling: "For the one in authority is God's servant for your good. But if you do wrong, be afraid, for rulers do not bear the sword for no reason. They are God's servants, agents of wrath to bring punishment on the wrongdoer." (Romans 13:4) In order to carry out this role, the state needs to collect taxes – and we, as citizens, are obliged to pay our taxes. (Romans 13:6-7) But it's important to remember that, biblically, the state is not the agent of mercy, but of justice. If government "stayed in its lane," our taxes would be significantly lower, and our society would be far less dysfunctional and divided – but more on that later.

Hence, as individuals, Christians are to deliver grace and mercy to gay, lesbian, and transgender persons; but they must also oppose—as representatives of the state—laws that deconstruct and undermine God-ordained and self-evident gender identity. To many, these different responsibilities comprise a horrible contradiction, and so they reflexively cry, "hypocrisy" and "bigotry," while venting their disgust at believers.

No doubt, these ideas seem mind-numbingly simple and obvious. If only that were still true in American culture, particularly among those who ascribe powers to the state that are biblically reserved for individuals, families, and the church. We have radically abrogated these distinctions, and somehow are surprised to find our familial, cultural, and spiritual foundations crumbling.

In short, many American Christians–not to mention unbelievers–have difficulty distinguishing between the distinct biblical roles of "citizen-ruler" and "individual." But discriminating between the two is of paramount importance, because many of our most vexing problems stem from this basic failure of discernment.

Is Jesus a Wealth Redistributor or a Supply- Sider?

Barack Obama famously touted the idea of, "spreading the wealth around." Karl Marx proclaimed, "From each according to his abilities, to each according to his needs." And Bernie Sanders observed that, "A nation will not survive morally or economically when so few have so much and so many have so little." All three have embraced, to some extent, the idea of redistributing riches from the wealthy to the poor.

But none of them is as radical as Jesus of Nazareth, who promised a near *reversal* in the status of the rich and poor in the afterlife: "So the last will be first, and the first will be last," he told his disciples. (Matthew 20:16) He further amazed them by saying that camels could pass through needles' eyes as readily as rich folk could enter into heaven. It was believed in ancient Israel that riches were the reward for righteousness, leading the disciples to wrongly assume the wealthy had an inside track into heaven. Jesus thoroughly squashes that idea.

Of course, it'd be unwise for anyone to assume he or she will get to heaven by virtue of an empty bank account. Poverty doesn't make one worthier of heaven, but it might make a person more sensible to their dependence on God and perhaps likelier to look to God for some big (hint, hint) spiritual need.

It would also be a mistake to think the folks at the top are excluded from heaven. But, they must–by faith–embrace inversion: "If anyone desires to be first, he shall be last of all and servant of all." (Mark 9:35) In short, the privileged are to release their grasp on money, power, influence, and fame and redirect it in service to Christ and others. If they don't manifest this fruit to any degree, their faith is a mirage.

Naturally, the great reversal Jesus talks of mostly concerns the exchange of material riches in the here and now for spiritual riches in eternity–what cynics like to call, "pie in the sky." According to Christ, many at the top echelons of power, fame, and fortune on earth won't have two wooden nickels to rub together in the afterlife, while significant numbers at the bottom rung in this life will enjoy vast heavenly riches. Indisputably, Jesus is a wealth redistributor.

Jesus illustrates the uncompromising nature of His redistribution plan in the parable of the presumably homeless Lazarus begging outside the gate of a rich man. After the curtain falls for each, the rich guy is in hell, while Lazarus lands in "the bosom of Abraham," a synonym for paradise or heaven. Tormented by heat and thirst, the rich man pleads with Abraham for a few drops of water, but Abraham responds:

> Son, remember that in your lifetime you received your good things, while Lazarus received bad things, but now he is comforted here and you are in agony. (Luke 16:25)

Hence, as a wealth redistributor, Jesus is far more radical than Bernie Sanders or Alexandria Ocasio-Cortez, both of whom would be content with mere income equality. In contrast, Jesus says that the condemned rich won't be equal in wealth to the redeemed poor, but will instead be completely *busted*! Conversely, multitudes of poor folk will possess an infinite and eternal spiritual endowment. And, unlike Bernie's redistributive plan, which has little chance of being enacted any time soon, Jesus' plan is bankable. He guarantees it, and since He kept that "rise from the dead" promise, His street cred is substantial.

Shock News! Jesus is also a "Supply-Sider" who Counsels that "Greed is Good!"

Those who interpret Jesus' proclamations on redistribution as a guide for social justice through public policy might give pause at another curious teaching by Jesus on wealth allocation:

> Whoever has will be given more, and they will have an abundance. Whoever does not have, even what they have will be taken from them. (Matthew 13:12)

The religious Left tend to overlook this scripture, which is eerily similar to their disapproving caricature of supply-side economics[1] whenever they are appropriating Jesus as a political ally. But this is tough stuff, even for conservatives, who aren't out to dispossess the poor *entirely* and give their assets to the rich, as progressives like to suggest. Talk about conundrums: this saying by Jesus appears to be completely at odds with His promise to redistribute from top to bottom. What gives?

We're not theologians, but to our ears, Jesus is saying that faith, repentance, and obedience in this life are rewarded with even greater gifts both now and in the future, while those devoid of faith ultimately lose everything– temporal and eternal blessings– when the final bell sounds.

Hence, Jesus primarily is talking about a different kind of earthly riches–spiritual

---

[1] Supply-side economics is a theory that a nation's economic growth can be stimulated by lowering personal and corporate taxes and decreasing regulation on businesses.

riches– which grow exponentially for those that believe in and live out the Truth. And, clearly, it's okay, and even encouraged, to have lots of these spiritual strengths and riches, which are the fruit of believing in and living for Christ, such as love, joy, peace, patience, goodness, kindness, faithfulness, gentleness, and self-control (Galatians 5:22-23). So, be greedy for them, He says. Indeed, this kind of greed is good.

Consequently, Jesus is both a wealth redistributor and a supply-sider, or at least the unflattering depiction of it by folks left of center. Which makes it impossible and unwise to infer that Christ's teachings on "redistributive" and "supply-side" economics were intended as prescriptions for governmental economic policy. In fact, the redistributionism of Jesus has little if any bearing on public policy, though many believe, and we would agree, that other passages and principles from scripture are relevant to public policy.

At bottom, the triune God ultimately is the Great Allocator and Redistributor of material and spiritual riches. Believers serve as His agents when they give to the poor. Yet, we are forced to accept an uncomfortable and politically incorrect conclusion: God does not ordain equality. Not that God is always pleased with inequality, especially when it is the result of greed, corruption, and oppression, but He leverages it for His own good purposes.

Scripture is unapologetic and relentless on this point: both now and in eternity, there will be great disparity between the haves and the have-nots, as regards both material and spiritual riches. Saying that out loud will anger egalitarians and universalists, but for the poor in spirit, it surely is great news.

We of course are commanded to help the poor and do all we can to ameliorate poverty. But we must do it with our own resources, not by establishing a "Robinhood" state that redistributes wealth from rich to poor.

Because God owns it all, He alone is the Great Redistributor of both material and spiritual riches.

Using one's vote to transfer money from wealthier citizens to poorer citizens essentially amounts to legalized theft. The state abrogates its rightful authority and plays God when it administers different justice based on how much money people earn.

The destructive consequences of our culture's radical departure from a biblical worldview are all around us, in the form of a slew of social pathologies that deprive children of the parental investment, modeling, and nurture that produces a productive citizenry. Ironically, by incentivizing dependance, inactivity and unwed childbearing, our government has greatly exacerbated income equality over time.

And, apart from a dramatic spiritual and moral reversal, America likely will continue rushing headlong upon this destructive path.

The Avariciousness of Government

When the different spheres instituted by God maintain their God ordained boundaries, humans are most apt to flourish. It's when these boundaries are over-stepped, and one sphere encroaches into one or more complementary spheres, that trouble begins. That's what we're seeing as the federal government transgresses its divine mandate, becomes increasingly invasive, and takes on responsibilities not its own. Not surprisingly, it ends up badly mismanaging them.

Socialism-friendly politicians, except when they're receiving generous honoraria and campaign contributions from Wall Street firms, love to rail against these firms. But to our knowledge, these firms, by making for their clients ample amounts of taxable earnings, are actually contributing significantly to the federal treasury. Nor are these firms burdening their clients with gargantuan debts. Quite the opposite.

If only that were so with our greediest of relatives, Uncle Sam, who since 2008, has added over 12 trillion dollars to the national debt, more than doubling it[2]. It now stands at a whopping 23 trillion dollars![3] Yet, in the minds of many, Wall Street is the personification of evil, and we and our elected officials are blameless and pure as ivory soap.

Contrary to the Left's claims, Americans are hardly hard-hearted. Twenty-six percent of our 4 trillion dollar federal budget went to healthcare programs, including Medicaid, CHIP, Affordable Care Act subsidies (Obamacare), and Medicare.[4] That's over

---

[2] Cox, Jeff. "That $22 trillion national debt number is huge, but here's what it really means." CNBC.com. https://www.cnbc.com/2019/02/13/that-22-trillion-national-debt-number-is-huge-but-heres-what-it-really-means.html?&qsearchterm=22 trillion national debt (accessed December 17, 2019).

[3] Just Facts. "Be Informed: National Debt." Justfacts.com. https://www.justfacts.com/nationaldebt.asp (accessed December 17, 2019).

[4] Center on Budget and Policy Priorities. "Policy Basics: Where Do Our Federal Tax Dollars Go?" CBBP.org. https://www.cbpp.org/research/federal-budget/policy-basics-where-do-our-federal-tax-dollars-go (accessed December 17, 2019).

1 trillion dollars per year, and it doesn't even include Social Security, which accounts for another trillion! Two trillion dollars total devoted to social welfare benefits! That's real money, as they say.

Yet, that doesn't even include what most think of by, "welfare"– direct payments to eligible recipients and food stamps. That eats up an additional 9 percent of our 4 trillion-dollar federal budget.[5] In other words, 59% of our gargantuan budget is for social entitlement programs.

Many still scoff at the "measly" 9 percent of the budget for direct welfare payments and food stamps, but by comparison, our entire national defense budget is only 15 percent of the federal budget.[6] In short, not even including Obamacare, Medicaid, and CHIP[7], we're spending 360 billion dollars on programs for the poor–roughly equal to the Gross

---

[5] Ibid.

[6] Ibid.

[7] Children's Health Insurance Program (CHIP) was signed into law in 1997 and provides federal matching funds to states to provide health coverage to children in families with incomes too high to qualify for Medicaid, but who can't afford private coverage.

Domestic Product of Malaysia or Singapore![8] More rational actors will acknowledge America's incredible generosity, and rightfully grieve the degree to which we're subsidizing marriage-less and fatherless communities.

But upcoming generations may not be so thrilled by our big spending ways, given how heavily it is funded by borrowing. As our children, grandchildren, and great-great-great grandchildren attempt to pay back our 39 trillion-dollar debt, the resulting fiscal austerity is likely to translate into a lower standard of living for them than we—the debt creators—now enjoy.

Notwithstanding, many on the Left will continue to paint "big business" as the enemy of all that is good and true, and Uncle Sam as our only defense against this wicked oppressor. Seriously, you can't make this stuff up!

---

[8] Statistics Times. "Projected GDP Ranking (2019-2024)." Statisticstimes.com. http://statisticstimes.com/economy/projected-world-gdp-ranking.php (accessed December 17, 2019).

But, at bottom, our fiscal woes flow directly from the conflation of sovereign spheres—in fact, the complete breakdown in the biblical lines of authority between Government, the Individual, the Church, and the Family. Let's be ultra-melodramatic and call it, "A Collision of Spheres."

ProofsandSpoofs.com isn't immune to the American tendency for hyperbolic sales puffery. We have to make a *very* small living, too.

In truth, it's really the case of one sphere ravenously gobbling up the others.

Classical Liberalism vs. Modern Political Liberalism

America's 50+ year love affair with big and increasingly intrusive government is especially ironic, since America was founded by a bunch of guys highly suspicious of government excess and abuse. Classical liberalism, in contrast to modern political liberalism, was forged in a centuries-long furnace of tyranny. The founders were acutely wary of oppressive and grabby government. So, they tyranny-proofed the new nation by devising an ingenious governmental architecture embodied in an "express powers" Constitution. If the Constitution doesn't specify governmental authority, the feds are forbidden from exercising it. Power is divided between three branches designed to check abuses by any one of them. Moreover, fundamental individual liberties are protected by an accompanying Bill of Rights, albeit not all were original beneficiaries to its provisions. It nonetheless contained the seeds of freedom for all.

But the Founders largely achieved what they set out to do: put a harness on government, thereby limiting its ability to interfere with the sphere sovereignty of individuals, families, and the church, while largely preserving the autonomy of state and local governments.

The encroachment of government upon these spheres has happened gradually, as the Legislative and Executive branches, with the permission of the Supreme Court, have transgressed the original limits of the Constitution, particularly by pilfering power from the States. In pursuit of the "general welfare," they've radically reimagined the Commerce Clause, vastly expanding federal powers.

The Taxman

A leading indicator of government encroachment is excessive and oppressive levels of taxation that hound Americans today–far lower levels of which sparked our separation from the British Empire.

It wasn't until May 8, of 2019 that Americans on average had worked long and hard enough to pay our collective tax bill (federal, state, and local) for that year, which includes taxes we'll pay in the future due to federal borrowing, according to the Tax Foundation[9].

Some will sniff at that and blame the rich for not paying their fair share. Yet the top 1 percent of earners paid 37 percent of the federal tax burden in

---

[9] York, Erica. "Tax Freedom Day 2019 is April 16th." Washington, D.C.: The Tax Foundation, 2019. https://taxfoundation.org/publications/tax-freedom-day/ (accessed December 17, 2019).

2016.[10] Moreover, lower-income Americans–those who make up the bottom 50 percent of taxpayers–paid just 3 percent of the total federal tax burden in 2016.[11] In fact, as of 2018, 44 percent of eligible taxpayers paid no federal income taxes.[12] Our tax system is hardly draconian in how it treats the poorest among us.

Yet, the highly progressive nature of America's expansive welfare state isn't sustainable. It is problematic because it ultimately presents citizens with a morally corrosive dilemma: Pay for entitlements, or benefit from them. And, while it's true all workers pay into the Social Security and Medicare funds, a great number of Social Security and

---

[10] De Lea, Brittany. "Here's how much wealthy Americans pay in taxes." Foxbusiness.com. https://www.foxbusiness.com/personal-finance/heres-how-much-wealthy-americans-pay-in-taxes (accessed December 17, 2019).

[11] Ibid.

[12] Stallworth, Philip, and Daniel Berger. "The TCJA Is Increasing the Share of Households Paying No Federal Income Tax." Tax Policy Center. https://www.taxpolicycenter.org/taxvox/tcja-increasing-share-households-paying-no-federal-income-tax (accessed December 17, 2019).

Medicare recipients receive or will receive benefits far exceeding their contributions.[13] The societal split between the "haves" and "have-nots" our entitlement system is producing is socially and politically polarizing, and a scary portent for democratic rule.

No matter; a robust cottage industry of neo-Marxists will continue to make a good living complaining about the rich being taxed too little. Naturally, it's smart politics, since the vast majority of voters aren't rich.

Hate on and envy rich folks all you want, but it's ridiculous to claim they're shirkers: the U.S. is more progressive than almost any other nation.[14] Even if the rich were taxed at much higher levels, the resulting revenue wouldn't come close

---

[13] Jacobson, Louis. "Medicare and Social Security: What you paid compared with what you get." Politifact.com. https://www.politifact.com/truth-o-meter/article/2013/feb/01/medicare-and-social-security-what-you-paid-what-yo/ (accessed December 17, 2019).

[14] Moore, Stephen. "Do the rich pay their fair share?" Washington, D.C.: The Heritage Foundation, 2015. https://www.heritage.org/budget-and-spending/commentary/do-the-rich-pay-their-fair-share (accessed December 17, 2019).

to covering our national expenses—there just aren't enough rich folk.[15]

Thus, our big spending ways necessarily inflict heavy financial pressure on the middle class: Americans collectively pay more in taxes than for food, clothes, and housing *combined*.[16]

All of which mirrors and validates the prophecy of Samuel, the rejected and broken-hearted Old Testament prophet who warned Israel about big government to no avail. As Israel discovered, trading God for government invites catastrophe and suffering. Sadly, it is a deal too many of us are quite willing to make.

---

[15] Bigman, Dan. "John Stossel: Tax the Rich? The Rich Don't Have Enough. Really." Forbes.com. https://www.forbes.com/sites/danbigman/2012/04/03/john-stossel-tax-the-rich-the-rich-dont-have-enough-really/#1a27f5b96e7d (accessed December 17, 2019).

[16] Hill, Catey. "Americans pay more in taxes than for housing, food, clothes combined." Marketwatch.com. https://www.marketwatch.com/story/americans-pay-more-in-taxes-than-for-housing-food-clothes-combined-2016-04-13 (accessed December 17, 2019).

The Holy Grail of Scandinavian Democratic Socialism

The American Left is currently under socialism's beguiling spell. Bernie Sanders and Elizabeth Warren want "Medicare for all," paid parental leave, free college tuition, and other benefits that presumably will move America closer to the democratic-socialist paradise of Scandinavia[1].

Let's give our friends on the Left a break and not mislabel what they hope to achieve. They are not proposing full-orbed Marxist socialism, in which the state forcefully seizes entire industries and eliminates private enterprise altogether. Equality out of the barrel of a gun, as practiced by Lenin, Mao, Castro, Pol Pot, Chavez, and Kim Jong-un, among others, has been a radically dehumanizing failure, particularly for anyone who dared resist it, resulting in

---

[1] Scandinavia is comprised of Sweden, Norway, and Denmark; the Nordic countries include these three, along with Finland and Iceland.

the murder and enslavement of hundreds of millions.

Sadly, Marxist totalitarianism continues to exist in places like North Korea and Cuba, both despicable and repressive regimes only an incurable communist could love. Fortunately, the heart's desire of the Left is the "soft" socialism of northern Europe, not the proletarian uprising and confiscation of private enterprise envisioned by Marx, although one could argue that Medicare-for-all proposals effectively nationalize the health insurance business and, in many ways, the health care industry itself.

Fortunately, socialist politicians in America continue (at least so far) to assert fealty to civil liberties, which gets lip service at best from Marxism's purists.

But what has Scandinavian-style socialism taught us? First, that the acolytes of European socialism haven't been paying much attention. The Nordic nations–Sweden, Norway, Denmark, Finland, and Iceland–have learned that extravagantly redistributing wealth is a jobs and economy killer. America's aspiring socialists are a decade, or two, or three, behind: Nordic countries of Europe have been moving away from socialism for quite some time, having gotten a taste of its bitter fruit. As a result, notes Swedish analyst Nima Sanandaji, "for the last two or three decades, Nordic countries have focused on market reforms, tax cuts, and welfare reforms rather than on continuing along the path of democratic socialism[2]."

Hence, these countries are far from the egalitarian nirvanas imagined by America's socialist dreamers, but instead free market economies with generous entitlement programs, funded by high taxes paid by everyone, not just the rich[3].

Sweden in particular made a decisive break from democratic socialism after experiencing economic stagnation,

---

[2] Sanandaji, Nima. "Europe's Welfare States Try Welfare Reform." Nationalreview.com. https://www.nationalreview.com/2016/08/nordic-welfare-state-failure/ (accessed January 6, 2020).

[3] Dorfman, Jeffrey. "Sorry Bernie Bros But Nordic Countries Are Not Socialist." Forbes.com. https://www.forbes.com/sites/jeffreydorfman/2018/07/08/sorry-bernie-bros-but-nordic-countries-are-not-socialist/#7bb3e4b674ad (accessed January 6, 2020).

crushing taxes, and "freeloader-ism." Despite frequently being hailed by the Left as a socialist exemplar, Sweden is actually a strong counter-example on the efficacy of democratic socialism.

In the 1970's and 80's, affluent Sweden experimented with welfare-statism on steroids, and paid for it with dramatic economic decline. During this time, the Swedish public sector grew massively,[4] and marginal tax rates as high as 85%, along with wealth taxes on personal assets, forced entrepreneurs, like the owner of IKEA, out of the country.

Sweden's socialist foray caused its economy to drop like a rock: Between 1970 and 1991, Sweden's GDP ranking dropped from fourth overall to sixteenth among Organisation for Economic Co-operation and Development (OECD) member nations,[5] having been surpassed

---

4 Zitelmann, Rainer. "Bernie Sanders Dreams of 'Scandinavian Socialism.' The Only Problem? It Has Long Since Failed."
https://www.forbes.com/sites/rainerzitelmann/2019/11/1 1/bernie-sanders-dreams-of-scandinavian-socialism-the-only-problem-it-has-long-since-failed/#95e58b86c5aa (accessed January 6, 2020.)
5 Ibid.

by European competitors England, France, Germany, Italy, and the Netherlands. Thanks to its socialist policies, Sweden "held the OECD record for the highest rate of non-working adults in the labor force for several decades.[6]"

Sweden awoke from its socialist nightmare in the early 1990's,[7] radically slashing income, capital gains, and corporate taxes. Since then, robust economic growth—well outpacing its European peers—has come back, and Sweden is now the wealthiest of all the major European Union nations.[8]

Corporate taxes in Sweden are lower than in America. Income taxes remain high, but are *far less progressive than in the U.S.*[9] The generous welfare programs

---

[6] Ibid.

[7] Ibid.

[8] Fernandez-Villaverde, Jesus, and Lee E. Ohanian. "How Sweden Overcame Socialism." WSJ.com. https://www.wsj.com/articles/how-sweden-overcame-socialism-11547078767 (accessed January 6, 2020).

[9] Pomerleau, Kyle. "How Scandinavian Countries Pay for Their Government Spending." Taxfoundation.org. https://taxfoundation.org/how-scandinavian-countries-pay-their-government-spending/ (accessed January 6, 2020).

in Sweden, including largely free health care and college tuition (room and board is not included) are paid by everyone. Even lower income workers in Sweden fork over nearly 50 percent of their earnings to the state: If you earn just $20,000 a year in Sweden, you only get to keep $10,600. Taking into account payroll taxes, which result in lower salaries, the effective tax rate on $20,000 of wages in Sweden is 62 percent![10] If that wasn't bad enough, Swedes also face a consumption tax (the "value added tax" or VAT) of 25 percent on most goods, excepting groceries, rent, books, and some other goods and services, which are *only* taxed at 12 or 6 percent.[11]

In contrast, 44 percent of Americans in 2018 paid a net of zero dollars in federal

———————————

[10] Neuvoo. Tax Calculator. Neuvoo.com. https://se.neuvoo.com/tax- calculator/?iam=&uet _calculate=calculate&salary=190000&from=year®ion =SMEDJEBACKEN (accessed January 6, 2020.

[11] TMF Group. "VAT in Sweden." Tmf-group.com. https://www.tmfgroup.com/en/services/companies/acco unting-tax/vat/country-profile/sweden/ (accessed January 6, 2020.)

income tax.[12] In fact, the bottom 20 percent of American earners have a negative income tax rate; they receive more from the government than they pay in.[13] It's hard to imagine that these Americans would prefer the Swedish system that has high taxes across the board, and where younger and healthier low-income workers subsidize the health care costs of older, wealthier, and less healthy Swedes.

We don't approve of burdensome taxes in Sweden or the U.S. But at least in Sweden, the government doesn't offer carrots for the poorest to remain in poverty: by taxing rich and poor the same, the poor in Sweden have no incentive to stay that way.

Moreover, Swedes recognize that their generous social services are only possible thanks to the golden goose of a thriving

---

[12] Fottrell, Quentin. "More than 44 percent of Americans Pay No Federal Income Tax." Marketwatch.com/ttps://www.marketwatch.com/
history/81-million-americans-wont-pay-any-federal-income-taxes-this-year-heres-why-2018-04-16 (accessed January 6, 2020).
[13] Ibid.

market economy–the very "goose" that the American socialists plan to suffocate with high taxes and regulation.

In short, America's wannabe socialists are true dinosaurs, seeking to replicate policies that failed abysmally in Europe.

We can only hope their ideas, like the dinosaurs, become extinct before a free and prosperous America does.

About the Author

David Culver Brenner is originally from New Jersey, where he attended Drew University and Rutgers University School of Law-Camden. After practicing law for several years, he worked as a grant writer for non-profit groups focused on strengthening marriage and fatherhood, including the Institute for American Values and National Fatherhood Initiative. More recently, he has been working as an English teacher and tutor, while writing serious and satirical essays on faith, culture, and politics for his blog-site, *ProofsandSpoofs.com*.

He lives in Northern Virginia with his wife, Kristen. Copies of this book can be ordered through *Amazon*.

About the Illustrator

Laura Graciela Lugo is a Venezuelan journalist, born and raised in Falcon, Venezuela. The crisis in her country forced her to put aside her profession as a journalist, and focus on her self-taught hobby, art. She now works full-time as an illustrator and graphic designer. She admires artists such as Salvador Dalí, Gustav Klimt, Francois de Felice, Max Ernts, and illustrators such as Lisa Zwerger, Gianluca Garafalo, and Quentin Greban.

She has illustrated 30 children's and poetry books. She can be consulted and commissioned regarding artistic endeavors via *Fiverr*.